THE BIG BOOK OF SEA MONSTERS
(SCARY LOOKING SEA ANIMALS)

BABY PROFESSOR

EDUCATION KIDS

The sea is famous for such bizarre wildlife.

Here are some of the scary looking sea animals in this world.

STARGAZER FISH

have mouth, nostrils, and eyes set high in the head. Stargazer fish bury itself in the sand of the area in which they lay their trap and will leave only their eyes unburied.

BROADCLUB CUTTLEFISH

is related to squid, octopus and chambered nautilus. Cuttlefish use color to communicate warnings, courtship displays, mood changes or for camouflage.

GIANT JAPANESE SPIDER CRAB

has the greatest leg span of any arthropod reaching 12 feet from claw to claw. The Japanese Spider Crab can be found in the waters of Japan.

OCEAN SUNFISH

is the largest bony
fish species. Ocean
sunfish can grow
as much as 5,000
pounds. Ocean
sunfish are found
in temperate and
tropical oceans
around the world.

SARCASTIC FRINGEHEAD

is a ferocious fish which has a large mouth and aggressive territorial behavior. Sarcastic fringehead have extremely sharp teeth.

WOBBEGONG CARPET SHARK

spend much of their time resting on the sea floor. They are mostly found in shallow waters around Australia and Indonesia.

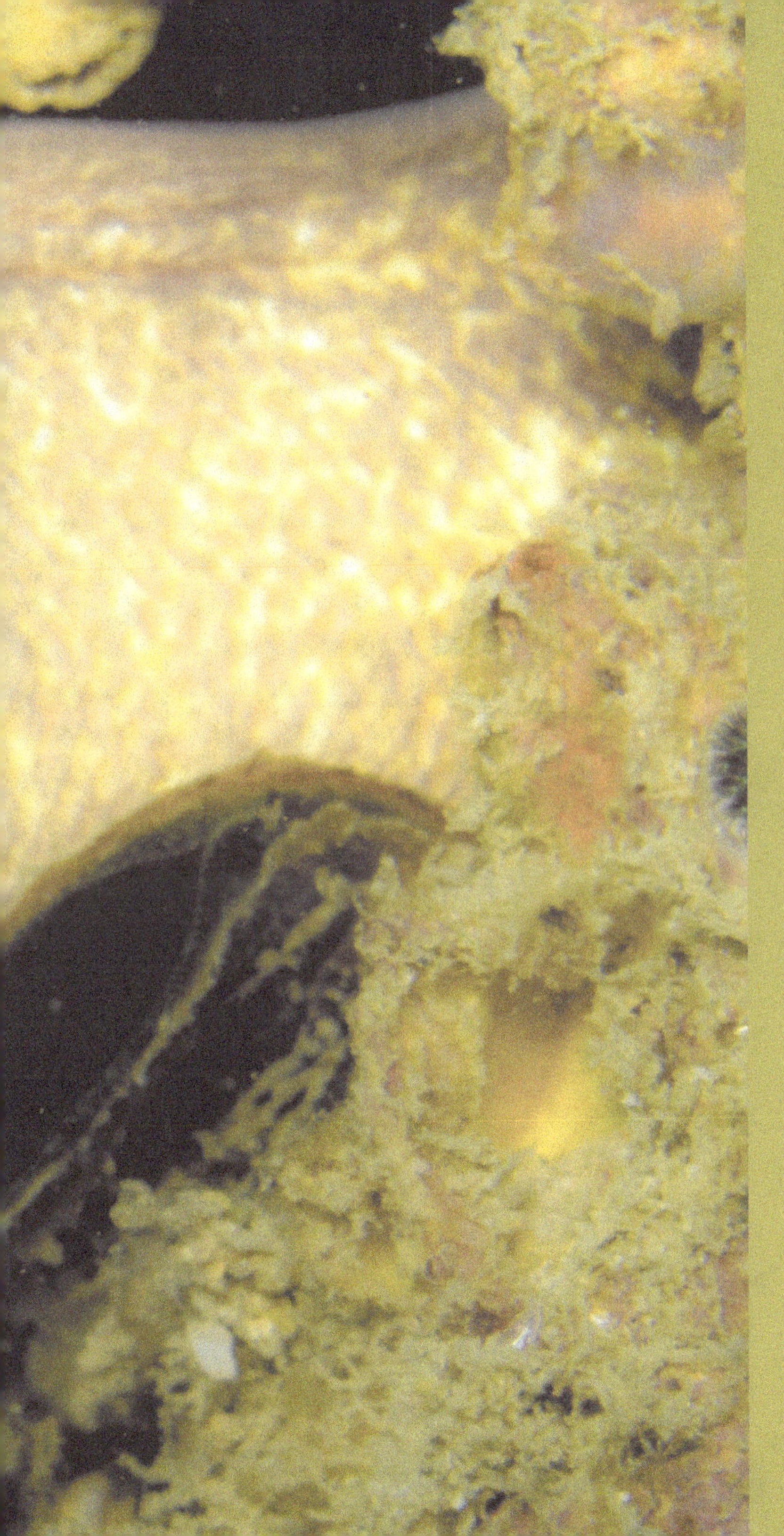

MORAY EEL

is the largest type of eel. Moray eel spends most of its time hidden in the caves on the bottom of the sea. Moray eel has a long and slender body which resembles to snake.